everything
in its
season

For the ones that believed in me way before
I was able to believe in myself

everything
in its
season

Lizzy Madrigal

ALEGRÍA

PUBLISHING

part I:
autumn

internal autumn

When summer turns to fall, we feel it in the crisp of the air and see it as greens turn to yellows. We are pulled to one another for closeness, our longing tying us together so that we won't drift apart. We seek the warmth of comfort as the world turns a bit colder. Within us, our internal autumn makes itself known by those similar tugs. As we near the newness of change, our minds turn us back to familiar comforts but our hearts push us forward.

Internal autumn is a bridge between what was and what can be, but only if we are willing to brave winter as we walk towards spring. To make it through this season means to choose courage, knowing that in order to become more we must embrace the pain of growth like an old friend.

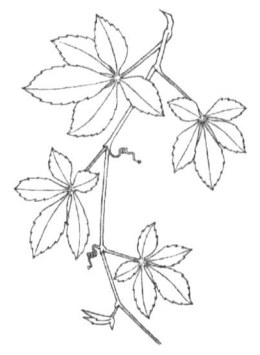

I hope you're able to catch the ways that your mind tries to lie to you. It's not to say that we shouldn't trust our thoughts, but rather, learn to discern when it's not in tune with our souls. Light and dark cannot coexist for long; one must eventually supersede the other. Even the happiest of us can fall deep into the dark pocket- but the good news is that we do not have to stay there. The mind is a garden; what you choose to feed grows. Do not stand in your own way and stop the growth that seeks you.

The rain is pouring down on the last hour of what was a very long, and emotional day. Days like these don't come around as often as they used to, which I am grateful for. But when they do... wow do they come full force.

So, what am I even talking about here? I'm talking about the days that begin with the sun and are later overrun by storms. Days that begin like any other day, but quickly stand out for all the wrong reasons. I woke up today feeling unrested and knowing that my choices would determine whether the storm would be unleashed or not. But I need to confess that I didn't make a choice. I let myself float through the morning, feeling the ripples of emotion crashing near the surface. But still, I ignored the warning. I grabbed my coffee, and mentally prepared myself for the day ahead, knowing that my inaction was a choice in the making. The rippling in my mind grew stronger, and the waves were getting bigger. I prepared my breakfast in an attempt to shut out the noise. Out of nowhere an outsider's voice broke through my thoughts and there it was: the explosion.

It was as though a bomb went off inside me, unleashing a hurricane of regret, pain, and sorrow. I was angry and I felt the familiarity of my brokenness. I did what I did best; I hid. I hid not to suppress my needs but because I still did not understand who I was in moments like these. Memories of previous storms flashed before me as I sank deeper and deeper into an abyss that I could not fight back.

Small. Insignificant. Irrelevant. Forgotten. These words taunted me and fed the unrelenting chaos that had overtaken my mind. The storm did not recognize the empathy or love I tried to pull in; instead, it continued to feed its hunger with my pain. The more pain it absorbed, the more satisfied it seemed, and I couldn't seem to stop it.

And suddenly out of the darkness, out of the clouds, and out of the storm, I felt a light. It was soft, inviting, encouraging, and loving. It reached for me and called me, waiting for me to call back. But I hesitated. I hesitated because I was afraid the words the storm spoke were true. And if they were true, how could I possibly be deserving of this light?

And then a new realization came: the light was part of me, just as the storm was. Both intense, both real, and both evidence of my humanity.

- Wednesday

There is more than one way to live a meaningful life. So many of us have battled with wanting to be seen, and in the process, we have compromised our identity and goals so that they fit with the unspoken narrative of what life "should" look like at different stages.

But that approach is so wrong.

Finding individual meaning means letting go of comparison; it means healing from childhood wounds; it means releasing people pleasing tendencies so that your mind and heart are free to be curious.

Meaning comes from doing things without the urge to seek approval from others. Meaning comes from slowing down and following your own timeline and not making decisions simply because "well, that's what you're supposed to do."

We've become more codependent and anxious than ever, because if we don't follow what everyone else is doing then that must mean there is something wrong with us.

And if there's one thing I've learned recently, is that that we long to desperately be seen as good.

But the truth is, we're the ones getting in our own way when we choose safe and predictable as opposed to taking on the pain of growth and individuality.

And perhaps that's what causes the ache in our hearts in the first place.

- more than one way

A while back I wrote this:

"Turns out the anxiety and depression were a misalignment between what my soul was craving and what I was actually doing."

Sometimes it feels safer to surrender to chaos than believe in the power of own thoughts and actions. We make it the master of our mind and therefore an easy target to blame, because blaming anything else is better than blaming our own selves.

So then we live in caution and fear, waiting for this invisible monster to appear unannounced and wreak havoc. We play life safe and, in the process, deny ourselves the chance at actually living.

I always knew I wouldn't be a young bride. And truthfully, I wish I would have shed the shame in that much sooner than I did. While other little girls shared their visions of happily ever afters, my head was in the clouds getting lost in daydreams that never really went away. I figured someday I'd catch up, but the only thing that changed were the goals that accompanied me in every stage of my life.

I wish I hadn't needed permission to be comfortable with my own companionship, yet I found myself justifying my decisions time and time again. I wish I would have had someone tell me that there was more than one way to live a meaningful life, but now I realize that person is me.

It's okay to have a vision for life in the same way that it's okay to wish for love. But to say it all must look one way is absurd; life is much too deep and significant to have one template. The only timeline that matters is our own.

- young bride

When my past visits me, she comes in the form of a young girl. She has my eyes, my smile, and she holds out her hand. I follow her and she shows me the early days of my life. I watch the ways in which my tender heart was formed, through scenes of my school days and the love I shared with my siblings. She replays my graduations and relationships, and the lessons that stayed with me in between.

When my past visits me, she comes in the form of a young girl. Whenever I see the sadness and confusion in her eyes, I try to fix it, but she stops me. "Patience," she says. Remember that this pain is temporary." So, I step back, and watch as her words come true.

When my past visits me, she comes in the form of a young girl. A new emotion comes to surface as I watch the pictures of my life: gratitude. I'm thankful for this tender heart and I'm glad I never threw it away. It's the evidence of a life well-lived, and it has so much more yet to give.

I think we need to stop referring to waiting as this monster that needs to be slain. We treat it like a dirty word that needs to be whispered versus shouted. Waiting is the thing that brings us pain while we're in it, and relief once it's gone. But what if we gave that pain a new name? What if we embraced it as part of our story?

There have been many times where I've wanted to rush through busy seasons, only to look back and wish I'd been more present. This is a reminder for me to slow down, and appreciate the way life looks now, because this moment is fleeting. But the truth is, that this is how life teaches us, without shortcuts and without previews. Each season leaves behind a lesson, but only if we are willing to look closely.

Once in a while I find myself replaying relationships that never were, wondering where I missed the mark. I think about what kind of life I would have had, and whether I would have been happy. It's funny how in certain seasons of our lives we are convinced that not having specific life stage markers disqualifies us somehow. At least that's how I felt at the time, despite not really knowing what I was even disqualified from.

Looking back, I see how I moved with a mixture of uncertainty and with an eagerness of wanting to prove myself. I attached myself quickly to the idea of someone, and blamed their insecurities and uncertainties whenever things did not go my way. I was eager for a man to see me and cherish who I was, but here's the thing: I was waiting for someone to do the one thing I could not do for myself. I never considered how I was showing up in those spaces; my head was just so focused on the constant rejection I felt.

But you know what, I'm glad it happened. I'm glad that the things I prayed for were delayed for me because I would not have known how to take care of a good thing. I had to learn how to face the reality of who I was and the hurt that I was carrying and projecting. I know now that not everyone gets a chance to face their flaws in solitude. I would even call it a privilege.

- delayed blessings

Sometimes I wonder if where I am is truly where God wants me

I've spent this first half of my thirties fighting off the sadness that has accompanied incredible highs

Every victory has casted a shadow, and sometimes that shadow blocked me from seeing the goodness of many wins

Even writing that feels so strange;

Because if something is good, shouldn't it be just good?

Or maybe that's a very naive way of looking at things because the reality is that life is not that simple

It's not black and white and it would be incredibly foolish of me to think so But God, is this where you really wanted me?

Watching on the sidelines as others continue to progress through life as they "should"

Am I behind? Or maybe an outlier?
Do I not get to live that too?
Am I to nurture adult hearts instead of children?
Do I pour my love into my life's calling instead of onto a husband?
Is that where you want me?

God, sometimes I wish you can write me a letter so I can ease the uncertainty of my heart

(But that wouldn't be faith now, would it?)

- letter to God, part 1

lizzy madrigal

part II: winter

An internal winter is a space within the heart that forms when we give fear a home. It begins with a light flurry that we don't think twice about, and so we go on about our normal lives. We look away for what seems like a moment and it's not long before we slip and fall and there's ice embedded in everything we feel.

And so we freeze. We will our minds to escape but escape does not come from the mind alone. The every thing that trapped us here is not the thing that will set us free. Praying for spring is not enough; but if we want to get there we have to have a mind that is willing to brave the storm first.

- internal winter

There's been a certain point in my singleness where my heart has felt quietly invisible. For years, I had watched from afar as friends entered different stages of life while I remained in the same place. Their titles became wives and mothers, and I was still just "friend." And the more that time passed, perhaps they became accustomed to seeing me as I had always been. But I couldn't help but feel that the way in which I moved in life was not as valuable as theirs. My fatigue wasn't like their fatigue, and my busyness was less than, because theirs had another human attached to it whereas mine did not. I have felt overlooked more times that I can count, because of the way that my life was panning out.

There is a certain version of loneliness that enters here in this mental space, in addition to a quiet hope that I will eventually be seen without really asking for it. But that's not how this works. They say that comparison is the thief of joy, and let's be honest, there's nothing to compare here and there never was. None of this was ever about who was getting it right or wrong, and I *wish* someone had pulled me aside years ago to help me understand this. There's beauty in the uniqueness of where I am, in the same way that there's beauty in the journey of the women around me. There is no race because a finish line doesn't exist.

Sometimes we're the ones solely responsible for creating the prisons in our minds that we are desperately trying to escape from.

Slow down. Posture yourself in humility. It's only by careful intention that we can avoid the pain of imprisonment altogether.

- an uncomfortable truth

There are two voices that whisper in my head at night, one protecting me from the chaos monster that visits at my bedside, and another that ushers me towards it. My mind is a battlefield and some nights I come out a tired victor, ready for the fight that the next night will bring again. But when I'm not, I'm the blind servant that follows the demands of the invisible monster until she's reached her fill. There is no in between; the choice is either to borrow love to get me through the night or allow the chaos to feed off of me.

- depression at night

I learned a lot about how I sought love by watching my mother. I explored her past and wondered why her pattern seemed to be one of unreciprocated love. In my early adulthood, I carried the burden of her happiness, at times at the cost of my own. Over the years, I have cried tears that she will never know about, ones that were caused not by the indifference of her family and friends, but by the realization that she was still yearning for her father's love.

My grandfather's indifference cast a shadow over a large part of my upbringing despite him never being present. The pain he left was suddenly mine the moment my mother taught me that to receive love, one must prove and earn it. My mother has never really known that to love is to remain still, and to be loved was a feeling of tranquility. Her version of love was always anxious, always loud, always saying "look at me, I'm here!" And if no one saw her, then it meant that she didn't do enough, didn't try hard enough, and that she herself was not enough.

But that ends here.

- Mother's inheritance, part I

I wish I didn't waste so much time wishing for the green pastures of what I perceived to be someone else's happiness. I, like so many others, spent so much time watching and longing for the curated versions of the lives that I saw online, wondering why mine looked so vastly different. I wish I could hold that version of myself closely, to remind her that different is okay. That I didn't need to compare my reality to others and mold my journey to fit the template of what I thought was a more valuable way to live. The truth is, I don't know all aspects of the highlight reels that I happen to see. Even the people that I know will always hold secrets that I may never learn, and I think it's a reality that we may not always acknowledge. A person's truth is limited to what they choose to share with us.

The digital world has a cunning way of preying on our lack. When we aren't feeling our best, we desire a distraction from reality. We scroll, filling our minds with narratives that other people have it better because they tell us so. So we feel behind. We feel less than. And before we know it, what was meant to be a quick distraction becomes yet more evidence of our incompleteness, all fabricated by partial truths.

- the social media monster

To the lovers that never were: I shouldn't have expected you to water my roses when I didn't do it on my own. I wish I hadn't put so much pressure for you to have desired me on my time, versus allowing you to discover me on yours. I allowed anxiety and insecurity to fill in the gaps for you, and my mistake was not letting you speak on your own. I know you saw the chaos, and I don't blame you for not wanting to take part of it. I see it now as a variation of mercy for both of us, really. I didn't know how to nurture my heart, and, in my desperation, I pushed all that out for you to fix.

But I promise you, I learned. I know now how to bloom on my own.

And I take joy in tending to my garden. I now seek the sun when my mood is overcast and I water my petals when I am in need of nurturing. I've learned to let go of the things that don't serve me, and release them like leaves in the wind. Rather than mourn what I may have lost, I whisper to my heart that it simply was not in season to receive. Until then, may I continue to give myself more time, more patience, and more love until that day comes.

Sometimes good people don't get what they want. In my seasons of longing, I recall how all my mind wanted to focus on was the one thing that I didn't have. I wasn't paying attention to the wins I was collecting; I didn't see how I was walking in the dreams of others, because all I saw was my jealousy for theirs. I guess what I am trying to say is that when we desire something deeply, all we see are the green pastures of other people's lives and we forget to water our own.

But that type of longing has starved and blinded me. It has disrupted my peace, its fed my own chaos, and in the end, never has it ever served me. Its only further burrowed me into the dark pocket of my mind, lying to me about how far I am from reaching the reward that I so wanted. In my hunger for happiness, I've disrespected myself and allowed the wrong people to have access to my heart. I was giving away what should have been earned, but my mind was blind and to relieve my pain, all I wanted was to eat from the wrong fruit tree.

Sometimes good people don't get what they want. But I think this is a lie; sometimes good people don't get what they want temporarily. When we are in a season of longing, it seems to have no end, right? I think our desperation takes us on detour after detour, unaware that we are the ones keeping ourselves from our happiness. Sometimes we don't get what we want because we don't sit still and listen. But how can we, when we've been taught that the only way to live is to constantly *get*? Forcing the body to run means the mind drags closely behind it, and if the mind is going, going, how can it stop us from eating the wrong fruit? How can we slow down and realize that the win we are chasing doesn't erase the wins we already have? And that there is how blinding ourselves is keeping us from the beauty that already is.

- slow down and wait

The thing that I don't dare say is that sometimes I resent the version of you that *she* got to meet. Her heart wasn't opened by you as mine was, but it wouldn't be fair to place all of blame on you. I chose to give my heart-my whole self- knowing no promises were given yet hoping that one day you'd change your mind.

But it doesn't quite work that way, I've learned. We don't have the power to love someone into changing how they feel about us. There is no formula for love, though we like to pretend there might be. The truth is, I need to let go of whatever feeling I've buried deep within me that resents the timing of when we met. I *wish* it would have been later. Then maybe I would have been able to cut out the mother wounds that got in the way of letting myself be loved. Or maybe that's wishful thinking. Meeting later wouldn't have guaranteed that things would have panned out the way I hoped they would.

That's life, you've said. Sometimes two people come together and they're out of season with one another. It's no one's fault, even though the heart wants someone to blame. But even when this happens, it doesn't mean there is no love at all. Love comes in many forms, many versions, and maybe, if we're lucky, we receive the thing we need and not the one we want.

- seasons of love

I arranged the tissue in the gift bag and carefully tied some pastel ribbons as the finishing touch. I paused to look at my work; this one felt a bit different. I've wrapped many baby shower gifts before, yet this one stirred up a mixture of emotions that I couldn't quite place. I was happy for my friends, there was no doubt about it, yet in that happiness there was some fatigue embedded. It embarrasses me to admit it, and it embarrasses me even more to make it the subject of a piece of writing. But I know that this combination of excitement and love and tiredness is one that many single women in their thirties experience. We just don't talk about it.

Over the years we have proven ourselves loyal and faithful, and good listeners to the friends that have become spouses and parents before us. We hear their woes, yet we can't relate but we remain as present as we can, anyway. Life's celebrations don't favor the person that's single, but rather, the person that adds to themselves through marriage and parenthood. Instead, we get well wishes and prayers that the tragedy of our singleness will end rather than prayers to be fulfilled and find peace in the season that we are in. Isn't it funny how that works out?

Why don't we gather for the woman that does extraordinary things? The one that buys a home, or builds a business? Or the woman that finally knows what it means to wait well? Why don't we gather for the one that learns to break the chains that she inherited? Most single women don't have the same network of support as does the engaged or married woman. Our work all done in silence, and alone. Yet we're expected to celebrate others' pivotal life moments with a smile on our face that doesn't waver. After all, eventually our "time" will come. At least that's what we're always told.

I've learned that those that call singleness a gift most times are not single themselves, and they didn't spend much time single. It's easy to give blanket phrases of encouragement to the woman in her twenties, but no one really knows what to say to the woman in her thirties when she is still waiting. Sometimes, friends and family stop saying anything at all. Maybe they feel strange? I don't know. But the silence is deafening.

What I do know is that the accomplished woman doesn't get checked in on often; in fact, she's the one that gets called on by the ones that need her. She's expected to pour and pour because she somehow always finds a way to refill herself.

I always do, I think to myself, as my mind comes back to the pastel ribbons. I pause to take a look at my work, releasing the emotions that were building up inside me. I grab my purse, my keys, and walk out the door with a smile on my face.

- pastel ribbons

Instructions on how to stop loving someone:

I. *(tell me how)*

I think we all carry an inner child within us, and often I'm reminded of her whenever I expect impossible perfection from myself. I think about how my words would sound to her ears, and immediately my language becomes gentle. I think about how my thoughts would fall on her heart, and my self-compassion kicks in. If I wholeheartedly believe that she is so worthy of my joy, then I am as well. If I am so adamant to protect this inner child within me, then I can do the same for the *me* that I am now.

I taught myself to bottle up anger and jealousy and I wore them like perfume

It was their scent that haunted my words, subtle, and lingering

"I'm okay"

"It's fine"

I couldn't stand to let you know that this part of me existed

I fought to control her, to bury her within me

Until one day I woke up and I just had enough

- perfume

Daughter, I have some words that I've been sitting with for a while. I wish I had the courage to have said this to you as a child, but perhaps I made excuses for myself because I was too afraid to face my truths...and for that I'm sorry. You see, it wasn't that I never loved you. I was hurting. And as a proud man, I hated feeling out of control with the love I had for your mother. But my God, she knew exactly how to push me to no end. She saw through the walls I put up; she was my mirror.

She reflected the worst parts of me and I couldn't stand to see the image of the man I had become. But pride was my master, and rather than taking responsibility for who I was, I deflected my shame onto you, my family.

Rather than heal myself, I sought easier women, and distracted myself with them. I created new families but I never forgot my first. I wish I had more time to love you the way you deserved and to tell you that there was never anything wrong with you. I'm sorry for the many times I turned you away when you cried to me. I hid my own tears from the world, knowing that I had lost myself in a storm of my own making, desperate to make my way back to what I knew was good.

But I didn't have the strength to, and that perhaps is my life's regret. When I did come close to making my way back to you, I chose the comfort of what I knew rather than the temporary discomfort to obtain something better. I thought about that moment often after that.

By the time you grew up, I honestly thought it was too late. But you had mercy on me. I didn't deserve your kindness, or your compassion in my old age. Yet, you showed up anyway. And you never stopped showing up.

You created a beautiful life, despite the invisible injuries that I left on your soul. You struggled, yes, but you persevered. You remained steadfast in conflict, in ways that I could never have. You're so much stronger than I, and I hope that in your memories, I'm not remembered by my mistakes, but rather, by the reconciliation that we achieved.

You made it, my sweet girl, you made it.

- things I wish my grandpa told my mom

A new season brings death to old ways. Yet it's not the death that we mourn but the loss of the skin that we shed. We fear the pain of release, without realizing that we've decorated past burdens as comfort. We whisper to ourselves "nothing changes until something changes" pretending the magic of transformation isn't in our hands.

Yet the wisdom of our past is what guides our steps. It is not the path that is new, but rather the awareness of a new us. The us that we have been patiently waiting and uncovering all along.

In opening my heart for the things that come next, I must first make space:

I'm letting go of feeling like an imposter
I have earned my way to be here, and my words need to be heard now.

I'm letting go of performing

Protecting the feelings of others is not my burden to bear.
I will speak freely when I am unsatisfied and speak love over the things that grow me.

I'm letting go of fear
This constant companion has been an opposer in my internal battles, but today she stays behind.

lizzy madrigal

part III: spring

I think that most of us carry the sunshine of an internal spring, the kind that triumphs through the thick of winter to remind us that perhaps we already have what we need to start new.

Here, the light intertwines with the dark; it's the place where discomfort meets hope, and where perseverance pushes and overcomes adversity in the same way a flower must push against soil to bloom.

It's the space in the mind where it delights in the fight to become more.

- internal spring

I've been thinking a lot about insecurity and comparison these last couple of weeks and so I took a trip down memory lane (as I normally do) whenever I can't seem to shake off some thoughts and/or feelings.

And I realized this:

I was probably eight or nine years old when I first had these things instilled in me. I was constantly compared to my cousins when it came to grades, height, sports skills, politeness, eating habits, and more. I was fed this idea that I was not enough on my own, and that I had to emulate others in order to be worthy or valuable. I know the adults in my life never dreamed of causing the pain that I still battle with today, but I'd be lying if I said there weren't days that I grappled with anger and sadness because of it. So now I am faced with a series of choices: do I blame others and remain stuck in this particular cycle of pain? Or do I make the choices that will bring me freedom from it? **The gaps in my confidence cannot always be filled by the affirmation or validation from others.** If there is insecurity in me, I must look at the ways that I believe I lack, and take action to become a better version of myself. If there is a habit of comparison within me, then that tells me I am not engaging enough in the things that bring me joy.

All in all, I have to move through my own life in a way that makes me proud of *myself* and for that there is no substitution.

- gaps

It's 6:30pm and I'm standing in my kitchen, adding a sprinkle of salt to what will soon become my dinner. There is the soft sound of a piano playing in the background, and suddenly I'm very aware of the cool floor beneath my bare feet. I look out of my third-floor windows and catch the last violet hues of an autumn sunset. The softness of the moment seems out of place for just a second. There are no children playing, no cartoons on the tv, no large dinner being prepared. And there's no husband coming home from work; just me in the stillness.

My heart begins to weep with grief for what is not here. But it's also weeping with gratitude for the things that are. Contentment and patience have become my friends. I've devoted myself to waiting well and it's transformed the way that I love. I've learned to embrace the small luxuries that life's gifted me, aware that I am living what other women long for and perhaps will never have. There is a strange feeling in holding both grief and gratitude in my hands, both flowing fiercely with lightness and heaviness all at once.

My mind dreams in hope and fears in heartache and I've never been a stranger to holding two opposing emotions at once. The heart is capable of such a task, and anyone that's self-prescribed 'big feeler' knows this. In a way, it's been my norm for years now; the outward expression of joy when celebrating others in contrast with the quiet longing that crept up in my solitude.

Yet here, in this space, the solitude does feel different. Here, in the life that I have built, there are remnants of joy that could have only happened in this season in my life. *I'm not late to this, I remind myself. I'm exactly where I needed to be today. And I'll be where I need to be tomorrow.*

My dinner continues to cook and my attention is brought

back to the calm of my apartment. I light a candle and set it on the dining table. I focus on the dancing flame for a bit, resting in the moment. For now, it's just me in this stillness, and that is everything. It's enough.

- solitude

Today I sat with the ugliest parts of myself. She is made up of sadness, anger, and jealousy, but has kind eyes. She speaks pretty words that aren't real, and her mouth is made of torment.

I invited her to sit with me because I was tired of her feeding on my joy. She didn't come quietly, but honestly, I didn't think she would. She likes it when I pretend she doesn't exist, but I know she watches me in silence until she decides to make herself known. For the longest time, I waved a white flag and begged her to let me have peace... but she'd already made a home in my mind. And maybe I let her stay because kicking her out was too painful. I didn't want to admit that I was the reason she was still here in the first place.

She agreed to sit with me, and watched me carefully, ready to bewitch me with her words. But I decided today our meeting would be different. I peeled her out of my mind, and she never stopped screaming as I did it.

And in the end, I was more than okay. I had finally done it.

The crack in the shutters let in the first glimpses of the morning sun, gently waking me. A soft orange glow broke through the darkness of my room, just enough to connect me to the promises of a new day.

I got up, stretched; my heart filled with gratitude for the body I was in. Recent autumns hadn't allowed me to be kind to myself, but that pattern was one that I was choosing to stop now. I had allowed myself to be stolen too long.

I am calm.

I am safe.

I made myself believe it. How can I go out and fulfill my purpose without showing myself my own love first?

I used to think I was an emotional oddity:

Desperate for attention but never willing to take up space
Ready to listen but never willing to speak

A walking contradiction always looking to find her place

Yet I learned that what I was experiencing was not an oddity at all

But a craving for permission to just be

A craving for opportunities to reveal my heart

And a desire to be truly seen

I learned that by relying on others to give me this permission

I was surrendering my own power and my own love

For there is no substitute for the permission that can only come from me

I have learned that there is nothing that can replace the treasure of a peaceful mind. In a world that readily sells stress and convinces us to buy, I've tasted the goodness of tranquility enough to silence the cravings of chaos.

I have learned that spectacle is the language by which to grab the world's attention, yet it leaves nothing but the aftertaste of emptiness. What good is a feigned performance that changes nothing? What good does a momentary rush of dopamine do if it leaves us the same? I've tasted the goodness of tranquility enough to silence the cravings of chaos.

I have learned that chasing highs will inevitably lead to lows. Life is meant to be a combination of both, yet human nature is calculating. We fight battles that are not our own and plead and beg for the universe to be good to us, but we can't bargain with life. We can't incite a battle and not expect to participate in the war. I've tasted the goodness of tranquility enough to silence the cravings of chaos.

- new treasure

I am still
I am silent
I am unseen

I am darkness
I am light
I am patience
I am fight

I am dreamer
I am lover
I am sister
I am friend

I am art
I am thinker
I am peace

I am silent
I am still

Last week, a friend asked me "When was the last time you felt truly happy?"

I had to sit with this question, because I felt an awkwardness arise in my chest for not having an immediate answer. Mostly because I think most people would, and they wouldn't "need a moment" for such a simple question as this. But I stopped my mind right there; comparison is never a winning game and if I am to keep my promise to love myself, that includes the way my mind thinks. Softly, I checked in with her.

She said this:

I'm done chasing happiness because happiness, like every emotion, is fleeting. Happiness is conditional on moments that don't last, and it is uncontrollable. Happiness is addictive; it can make us chase cheap highs in order to keep up with the perceived 'happiness' of everyone else. But like all highs, it must come down. I'm more concerned with what's there in the aftermath of that happiness. Is it chaos? If it is, then happiness is just an escape, isn't it? But if it's peace- and I hope it is- then that is more constant. In my younger days, I chased perceived happiness but in my wiser years I choose to pursue peace. Peace is not fleeting; it's steady and calm, and it doesn't make me wait for the next time I'll see it again.

Be careful to not be so consumed with being perceived as "good" that you lose yourself in pretending you have no flaws.

Vulnerability is no different from nakedness; reveal who you are and let the world choose to love you or not.

But in the midst of that, choose to love yourself anyway.

I'm sitting near a large window in a house by the North Sea, watching an old man play fetch with his dog. Above him the clouds are a dark gray, with slivers of golden light shining on the trees behind them. The scene looks like a postcard frozen in time.

This moment itself feels a bit surreal. I think about the combination of moments that must have aligned perfectly in order to have brought me here to this corner of the world. My mind wonders about the thousands of strangers I pass when I'm in places that aren't home. I question who they are, and why they're in such a hurry. I wonder if they're having a good day, or if they've just received news that's changed their world. They could be having the worst day of their life and none of us would know.

Every one of them holds a universe that we only get to know for mere seconds. It's amazing how much I realize I miss out on when I don't make the intention to slow down. Perhaps a break from the norm of hurry is what the mind needs from time to time...A break that allows space to notice the little moments like an old man playing with his dog by the seaside.

- Sitting in Kent

When I was a child, I accidentally learned that to be busy was to be worthy. When I was an adolescent, it was *confirmed* to me that to be busy was to be worthy. When I became an adult, I eventually learned that to be busy required the sacrifice of the things I loved. To be busy meant achievement, to be busy meant status. But in reality, "busy" meant the sacrifice of my peace and eventually that became too costly. So, I killed the "boss babe" because she was asking for too much. I learned to slow down and invited my softness to make herself known. With patience and love she has shown me how busy became a distraction from the things that I was afraid to face. Busy didn't mean worthy...it meant pretending to be okay. Busy was a way to hide that I felt insignificant and small. There was no status in this- so I shed that hard shell and allowed a new version of me to bloom.

Busy is no longer one of my invisible masters. Instead, I lean on the wisdom that only slowness can bring. I've become tender and more gentle with myself in a way that allows me to express myself without the chains of restriction and fear that bound me before. The noise is gone; and all that remains is the fullness of who I choose to be.

- killing busy

I sat at a café near my house once, watching people pass and enthusiastically distracting myself from writing pages. Out hurried a young woman, no doubt racing the clock and a to-do list ringing loud in her mind. From behind, her head was slightly slanted as if looking at the door handle. Push. Nothing. Push. Nothing. Push. Nothing. Sighing and flustered, she turned around and walked out the back door. I glanced at the door: it said pull.

She didn't notice, despite her eye level being seemingly aligned with the door sign. I think if she had just taken a moment to pause, after the first or second try she could have corrected her mistake. Instead, she allowed defeat (and perhaps embarrassment) to take the win. This little encounter made me think: how often do we move about life this way?

Would we be willing to not push away discomfort, if we knew it would get us to the destination that we wanted? Or, if we slow down, we could adjust ourselves and pull towards what's meant for us?

Someone asked me recently for some tips on self- love, so I told her this: give yourself permission to not like who you are right now. If you want to love yourself genuinely, start by being honest with the things that need to change, and love yourself enough to do them. If you don't do what's necessary to receive your own love, you'll have a hard time receiving anyone else's.

Time is a wise being that makes no mistakes
What we once waited for in the darkness
Will now be our gift in the light
Sometimes we fear waiting because we lose hope that our
wish will never be ours to receive But time reminds us that
in our waiting we ourselves became the gift that we will
give to the lover that we have anxiously prayed for

I realized recently that in order to **become** better than I was yesterday, I have to make the choice today and every day to be curious about my everythings. It is through the softness of my heart and the gentleness of my mind that my truest self will flow.

The mind is a garden; whatever I choose to water is the thing that will grow. If I nourish the roses of purpose, they will bloom. If I nourish the lilies of peace, they will flourish. Yet, if I choose to give my attention to the weeds of jealousy, or those anger, then they too will grow.

Every choice either feeds or starves the garden; and it is on no one but me to decide what thrives.

I think I'm ready to stop feeling shame for longing companionship. No frills, no spectacle; just the calm, steady, presence of someone that I know has me covered. I'm done feeling bad for not wanting this sooner. I'm through with the guilt of my past immaturity. Life has brought me here by way of this path and I'm openly declaring my love for how it turned out. Longing is not a wasted emotion when it is rooted in love, I don't think. As I've grown myself, I've planted seeds for new desires. In due time, the fruit of my waiting will arrive when it needs to.

At the end of my life, my only desire is to know that I was able to bloom to my fullest ability wherever my feet were planted.

To leave behind every ounce of my love and compassion, knowing that I would not need it with me where I'm headed next.

On the day that I lay on my deathbed, I wish to not mourn the memories that I didn't make time to make.

Regret shall not be my companion, because I have seen what it does to regretful hearts.

But life doesn't give us warning; I am not guaranteed the luxury of knowing when I go.

So I'm left with no choice but to bloom wildly every day, even when I don't have the heart to do
so.

So God, I pray my hands are blessed to choose to show up even when my mind is unwilling.

I took a walk today and I thought about the blessing of solitude. As I near yet another birthday, I can't help but think that this isn't exactly how I had pictured my life. I thought certain things would have happened by now (you know, the things that everyone says we must do) but my reality is that those things have not happened yet. And honestly, there is no guarantee that they are. And I ask myself: can I make peace with that? There are days where it's hard being an outlier amongst friends and family, yet there are other days where I cherish the blessings that come only by living alone. The truth is, there will be a time where I may miss the version of me that exists now. And what a waste it would be, if I spent it questioning the future instead of living in the fullness of what's in front of me.

- quiet blessings

What would I do if I were free, truly free?

Well firstly, the bruises on my ego would finally erase because I'd stop beating on myself so much. The language of my mind would soften, and I wouldn't be so afraid of embracing my shortcomings, wondering why I let them get there in the first place.

If I were free, I'd assume the best of myself without a second thought to who I was performing for.

If I were free, I'd wrap myself in tenderness and crown my head with unconditional love, the way a new mother embraces her child.

What I've learned about freedom is that it's a daily choice. The very same thoughts that harmed my mind are the ones that hold the power to heal and free me from the prisons of my own creation.

The door to my freedom has been open all along.

Last week I boarded a plane and overheard a conversation happening in the row behind me. The voices belonged to two men, probably in their late twenties, who were excitedly sharing with their neighbor that this was the first flight for one of them. She happily joined in their excitement, and when her disbelief came, she asked why it had taken him so long to fly. "There just wasn't an opportunity," he said simply. And that was that.

I sat with that exchange, mindful of my own reaction to hearing someone engage in something like this so late in life. But I stopped myself there; what about this qualified it as *late*? Why do we- including myself- keep categorizing certain experiences into timeframes by which we need to do things? I don't know anything about this man's story. Perhaps he didn't have the financial means to do it, or maybe he was just not interested in flying before- which is *valid*. He is allowed to do things on his time, and you, whoever you are, reading this, are too.

Do not allow others to convince you that everything in life worth happening can *only* happen in our youth. New beginnings are just as beautiful at sixty as they are at twenty. Whatever you didn't experience in your teens doesn't lose value just because you experience it a decade behind everyone else. Let's stop pretending that life ends at thirty, or forty, or fifty. It ends when it ends, and until then it begins new with every sunrise.

- first plane ride

A note for the ladies: When you feel insecure about yourself, it is not the responsibility of a man to calm that chaos for you. No man or person can love an insecure woman into becoming secure; this change can only come from within herself.

And it comes from being brave enough to admit that we are flawed. Some of my biggest victories have come after long nights of tears, where I take a deep look at myself and accept that I am here because of the decisions and habits that I created. Does that make me a bad person? No, just flawed, same as everyone else. But awareness isn't enough. To be free, to create change, we must love ourselves enough to not remain the same. To be confident is to love the version of you that's in progress, despite the imperfection. It is then that you open the heart to be loved in return.

This is how I am learning to prepare myself for the love I seek.

Sometimes I wish I could take the hand of the girl I once was and tell her to slow down To not worry about making everybody happy without a second thought for herself

To not feel pressured to perform in exchange for affirmation

I wish I could tell her to save some of what she gives just for her

It wouldn't make her selfish, and it wouldn't make anyone angry

She never had to be perfect

She didn't have to play make believe, or mold herself into anyone's dream girl I wish I could hold her hand and tell her that she was enough as she was

That she was exactly where she needed to be

- enough

In order to make space for the new, we must learn to part ways with the old, and break our own hearts in the process. We shed our old skin, peeling it away layer by layer until we find ourselves naked in front of the mirror, desperately searching for the new person hiding within. Building a new life is like planting a garden; it cannot be done on rocky terrain. In pain we remove the weeds, pulling at our souls until we feel almost empty. With despair we then sow the seeds, anxious for the flowers to come. But that is not enough for the bloom to be guaranteed.

A garden needs to be nourished for its body to grow; it cannot be rushed. It must be exposed to the sun and be brave enough to withstand it. A garden needs a green thumb to show up every day, even if it's just to watch it from afar, and in silence. And then at the end, when all the patience, and all the nourishing, and all the bravery come together, again, and again, and again...it is then that it dares to bloom.

- *change*

I've noticed that sometimes we do this little dance where you find yourself having to remind me just how much I mean to you.

I think I just want to be special in your life and my desire for that has clouded my ability to see all the ways that I already am.

- special

I used to call myself "lonely"

But the older I get, the more I realize that loneliness may be a symptom of a disengaged soul

It's an accumulation of self-denial, of misplaced self-love

A result of floating through life and letting it happen to me instead of *for* me

But as I learned to understand my mind and heart more

I realized that the very same way I drove myself to a place of loneliness was also how I could lead my mind back to reconnection with my heart

It may have taken me a few wrong turns to get here, but I got here

And *here,* my heart recognizes the treasure I was seeking was within me all along

- lonely

In my new season, I am no longer afraid of getting older. I picture myself sitting every morning at my kitchen table, free and light, letting my words flow without evidence of hesitation and doubt. I picture my actions rooted in assurance of who I've molded myself to be. The deadlines imposed on me in my young adulthood suddenly don't matter as much. The template of what makes a "good life" is no longer relevant to the person I have become and continue to choose to be. There's freedom in letting go of expectations of the past in order to make space for the now. But first we must have the courage to release what keeps us small.

I hope to receive whatever comes next with a grateful heart
that doesn't forget the journey it took to get there.

part IV: summer

An internal summer burns with yearning and excitement;
It bursts us open to joy
To curiosity
To passion
It ignites the wildfire within us that burns into a glorious obsession, covering us with boldness to act and fearlessness to dream.

- internal summer

Everything you've ever wanted and hoped to be is on the other side of courage. Learn to befriend discomfort, even if it takes a while. You may just find yourself pleasantly surprised at what you're capable of when you let yourself be uncovered by the unknown.

The sooner we can accept that we are imperfect and own our mistakes, the sooner we can stop spending our energy trying to prove ourselves and just be. When we feel pulled to argue and prove, we are functioning from a place of lack and uncertainty. True empowerment is admitting wrong, not convincing others we are right.

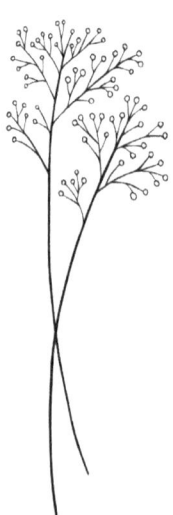

You may desire all the beautiful things for someone with every ounce of your being, but none of it matters if they don't open themselves to the possibility of more.

Do not beg people to accept the goodness of your gifts knowing they will not be kept as treasures.

Do not pour into people who do not wish to return the same to you.

A giving soul needs nourishment to flourish, in the same way a sunflower needs the light of the sun to thrive.

I say this with love:

Sometimes we exaggerate our situations by adding unnecessary emotions. Remember, those are fleeting.

The more you make friends with discomfort, the more room you make to tap into the fullness of who you are.

A large part of being unable to wait well is fear-based; we act prematurely because we fear that nothing better will come along.

But waiting for something to happen is a passive approach to life.

Nothing changes until something changes. Life is happening today.

In the morning, before your feet even touch the ground, you've been chosen to be given a thousand miracles in one day.

The process of stopping to take a breath is a miracle.

The function of your lungs is a miracle.

The beauty of your consciousness is a miracle.

Being alive is a miracle.

And yet, it's so easy to think of a thousand reasons why we are not enough and/or don't have enough.

Let this note be a reminder: You are an infinity of treasures.

And your miracles are waiting for you.

- A thousand miracles

The flower lives many lives
She begins small
And she doesn't think twice about what her neighbor
may say about her
She grows with the help of the sun and the rain,
Never once questioning whether or not she deserves their
help
She accepts it with ease in her spirit and grace in her stance
Dependent she is for a while, unapologetic
Until one day she has strength to bloom on her own
And bloom, she does
Until one day her short life sees its last day
But as she wilts, she still offers a gift:
She leaves her fruits as she departs
But again, she returns, seeking the sun and the rain
Her beauty blooming and undeniably gracing nature with
her existence.

-Lessons from flowers

Reminders for when you need to take care of yourself:

- Slow down
- Enjoy the scent of your coffee
- Light a candle
- Stand in the sun
- Believe in your capabilities
- Send a voice memo to a friend
- Listen to the soundtrack of your favorite movie
- Buy flowers
- Take a bath
- Take a rain check
- Hug somebody close
- Go for a walk
- Say thanks, even when you can't think of what for

To the brown-skinned girls:

May your feet take you places where your ancestors couldn't

May your eyes see a world with a place for you in it

May your mouth not be afraid to ask for what you are worth

May your hands create spaces for our future girls to belong in

And above all else, may your heart forever be unwavering.

Your name has been familiar to my soul for more than six thousand days, and despite the pauses over the years, my heart continues to be tethered to yours.
Even in seasons of unfamiliarity and distance, it's your name that my being responds to.
It unlocks memories of a time before life became harsh; a time when all our fantasies still had a chance to come true.

- friendship

Soft love is the most underrated love, in my opinion. While others may need spectacle, for me it was the quiet, thoughtful moments that did it-

It was the way you knew I'd love bookstore hopping after we had lunch for the first time. It was bringing lactaid before every brunch to ensure I'd be able to enjoy my meal. For me, it was your patient voice that reassured me the first time I cried in front of you. It was the way you playfully tugged on my hair, knowing it drove me crazy (in the best way). For me, it was the scent of your skin lingering on my sweater after a long hug.

I noticed that one of these moments were particularly loud. They were all small moments. Yet, when we think about what makes life precious, it's the culmination of millions of small moments like these, all intertwining with each other by mere chance. Perhaps it was an accident that we found each other...but I'm starting to think it was no accident at all.

- soft love

One day I hope to look over at you and take note of the way my heart swells at the thought of the million little moments that led us here. I hope that I hold onto the lessons brought forth by the pain of waiting and being shaped by the "nos" I encountered… None of it an accident; all carefully crafted by God.

A good lover isn't defined by how he touches my body, but rather by how he listens to my soul. His presence is gentle yet firm, unmoved by the chaos of my mind or the worries of my heart. His hands don't move solely for pleasure, but to reassure me that he's here to stay. Remember: A good sex partner is easy to get, but a good lover is a treasure to be found.

You are "stranger"
Sometimes I sit and think about all the people I pass, whose lives I don't know until one day, by a small chance, I will. I wonder how many times we must have driven down the same streets, not knowing we'd meet years later.

You are "friend"
Your precision in how you understand me is unnerving, yet I continue to hold the door open to invite you in. My curiosity swells as I watch your words uncover me, intrigued by where our path will lead.

You are "lover"
Your name in my mind rings like a poem. You've redefined my understanding of intimacy: I've come to know my own being alongside getting to know you. It's not just my body that has found home in you, but my heart too.

When I think of you, I think about your heart before anything else

Though the beauty of your look is captivating, and the curve of your smile enticing,

It's the light of your eyes that loses me in the only place that I have ever desired to be lost

The more healthy and emotionally sound you are, the more people want to take from you. Be careful who you give yourself to.

Not everyone has earned the privilege of your time.

- Morning conversations with friends

When I make a decision to love you,
I choose to love ALL of you
And I will not opt to back down when things get difficult
I hope you'll be able to help me rise when I fall
In the same way I will extend my hand towards you when you need it most I will not choose to see you through the lens of your worst day
And I hope that you will be here through mine
I hope we don't lose sight of our rhythm
Or refuse to listen when our faults become worn like masks
In those moments, I hope we can reach that place beyond words and steer away from silence For silence is surely death
I choose to believe in the love that I chose
The love that encapsulates ALL of who you are
The you I met yesterday, the you I see today, and the you that you will become

I want to walk hand in hand with you
And feel the warmth of your skin against mine
I want my body to shrink into yours
And feel the gentle beat of your heart grow faster
I want to feel your kisses
Your lips inviting my soul to intertwine with yours

I want to be one with you,

    and stay

       in this moment

          for all of time

There are no words to describe what's it's like to sit with somebody who holds you steady with
their presence as the chaos in your mind makes it seem like everything's about to fall apart.

Welp, here I go again, I think to myself. No one wants a part of this, so this is where he lets me go.

But it didn't happen like that. Instead, he was quiet. Patient. Calm.

He let me take a moment to think, so I can articulate the contents in my head instead of just
pushing them away as I typically did.

Today I didn't have to pretend like I wasn't upset. I had permission to be as I was.

He gave me room to be how I needed to be, and eventually I found my way back.

I was seen.

- presence

Perfectionism is painful. Give yourself permission to not like who you are for a bit and choose to do something about it. Don't be afraid to sit with those ugly parts and love them unconditionally anyways. You don't need to perform anymore.

10 things I've learned while being in my 30s:

1. Age is an illusion.
2. You'll change your mind about what you want in life, maybe more than once. That's okay.
3. People will disappoint you; let them.
4. People will love you on a different level; let them.
5. The things we were told would bring happiness to our lives won't guarantee that happiness.
6. Joy becomes more important than happiness, and it'll find you in small, unexpected ways.
7. Peace of mind is the most important currency.
8. Stillness becomes more valuable than spectacle.
9. There is no deadline for anything; throw timelines away.
10. A fulfilling life begins with a healthy mind and a healthy heart.

What I know about love today is....

That it's not about the flower count in a bouquet, how many times I'm taken out to candlelit dinners. It's not about the gifts I receive or being told I'm pretty every day.

Love is the care that is shown in little moments that can be easily missed. Love is paying attention. It's the way someone walks on the outside to protect me or knowing my orders to the same three restaurants I go to because I'm a creature of habit. It's walking into my home and fixing little things here and there, just because they can. It's bringing me dinner because they know I'm working late. It's taking a video of a cat in a window, simply because they know it'll bring a smile to my face. Love pays attention.

Love is soft, and peaceful, like a gently flowing stream. It's kind, patient, and on time.

"Allow yourself to be enjoyed."

I don't think he realized how he touched me by saying the words he did. I had playfully blocked
his compliments and brought negative attention to the sweetness of my palms instead.

I don't know why I couldn't just be.

Perhaps it was a way to protect myself; believing that anyone would delight in the presence of
my company seemed so far-fetched. But it wasn't.

I think this realization made it all the more sad, because I knew that somewhere, deep down, this
negative self belief I was so desperately trying to shed. I was hungry for these types of words, for
proof of my worth, for a watering of the garden within me.

But growth doesn't happen without love. It's what inspires growth. And the more I longed for
nurturing, the more I realized I was desiring something that had been accessible to me all along.

And maybe, just maybe, if I were kinder and gave myself the thing I was desiring, then I
wouldn't be so quick to decline the love that other people wanted to give me.

After all, beauty attracts beauty.

You cannot offer yourself partially to the world and expect to be loved fully.

I remember the night I discovered your curiosity for me

The delicate weaving of your words set my womanhood aflame in a way I didn't know it could

"I have to undress your mind before your body" you had said

And I have never craved to be naked as I did then

I wanted to memorize the melody of your words

And when I finally felt your touch, a symphony erupted from my body

You filled me with the beauty of your masculinity

Forever to carry the evidence of your art

He asked me:

"What would you do if I died?"

I replied simply, "I'd be heartbroken forever."

I think he thought I was being too kind, because he followed up with "Really? I think you'd eventually move past it."

Maybe he was right. But in that moment, there was no way to tell him that just the idea of him gone made my heart shatter into a million pieces.

The dark was never an association I had with friendliness or
anything kind
   Until I began to shed myself within it

I threw out my old thoughts, my old ways, and the smallness
of how I carried myself

I removed my mask and eventually my clothes
   Desperate to be truly discovered entirely

Night once represented loneliness but eventually it was
where I met curiosity

Your midnight eyes watched me and I relished in their
attention
   And in the dark I began to change
    I made myself naked and ready to claimed
     Opening myself while exploring the hidden
     depths of my person

Gentle fingers caressed and traced every part of my skin
Until I unlocked the part of me that I had hidden away years
before

Now I eagerly I wait for those midnight eyes to watch me
come into myself
   Again
     and again
       and again

- midnight eyes

The other night I dreamed I was seventeen again. I was walking the halls of my memories, looking through a life that seemed to have only lasted a blink of an eye. I tried to remember this version of me, a child really, at the cusp of a great change without the slightest idea of how it would go. I remembered the taste of fear in my mouth and the sound of confusion in my ears, nervous to enter a new season of my life. But as I stared at the face of my youth, I wished nothing more than to comfort her and remind her that she needed not to worry about her future self; her present self was the one that she needed to give her love to; it was the only way to bloom. And that was enough.

Yet, I wish I would have spent more seasons of my life focusing on watering myself for growth versus focusing on just blooming. I wish I knew what I know now: that the beauty of the journey is the hardship that we experience as we uncover new versions of ourselves; that growth wasn't something to rush through, but rather, a privilege to experience.

But of course, there is no awakening to this knowledge without having lived some life first. We don't get the benefit of foresight because in doing so, then we would act with the intention of receiving the outcome that we think best suits us. But that isn't living. My proudest moments have come from rediscovering hope after failure and delays. It continues to come from intentional waiting, overcoming internal struggle, and choosing to move forward regardless. This is what refines us. This is what creates a blooming life.

I met my daughter in a dream once
She was Mia, as was her name
My heart was in her eyes
      and somehow I knew her smile was her father's
She looked at me like she'd known me her entire life
      yet I had only just met her here in this dream world
I could feel her small hands in mine,
      wondering if I'd ever feel them earthside

When I woke I still felt her with me,
      and sadly I haven't seen her again since
But every once in a while I think of her
      my girl, my Mia,
      and wonder if she's still waiting for me to return again

- Mia

November 4/ June 17/ August 6/ December 27/ you're forever ingrained in my memory/ oh look at you/ who are you?/ gosh you're loud/ I think I love you anyway/ mom and dad look more busy now/ here's another one/ and another/ I think this is the last one/ I can help mom now that I'm a little older/ I love him so much/ I love my sisters so much/ maybe I can dress them up like dolls/ you're growing so fast/ we're growing so fast/ oh look, we're older now/ *time, please slow down/* one day it won't be like this anymore/ if anything happens to you, I will die/ I never get tired of playing with you in our backyard/ but eventually did we did stop and we had no idea that was the last time/ when did we stop playing?/ four quinceañeras and four graduations have passed/ my youngest sister is talking about moving away and my heart is breaking/ she's done it, I'm so proud of her/ I see her often and it brings me so much joy/ my other sister is dating, I think he's the one/ my other sister is following her dreams/ my brother is young but I love our relationship/ my youngest sister is back, I'm so happy we're all together again/ my other sister is sick, I'm scared for her/ she's okay, everything is okay/ we're getting older/ *time, please slow down/* my other sister is married, she's moved out now/ we feel incomplete and complete all at once/ my other sister is talking about moving, my heart is breaking all over again/ she's done it, I'm so proud of her/ maybe I should have gone too/ I blinked and we're all adults now/ *time, please slow down/* my sister is back, I'm so happy/ life is happening so fast/ we're getting older and things are feeling more serious/ what do we want?/ what is it that we were put on this earth for?/ now my brother is talking about moving away and my heart is feeling that familiar sensation/ everything is happening in cycles/ it's good, it's bad, it's good again/ things are harder sometimes but we always find a way through/ I'm loving you more every day and I don't know what tomorrow will bring but I'm still here/ for you and you and you and you/ I'm forever here/ forever ingrained in your memory for however long life will allow us

- for my siblings

for my parents:

I can't imagine what it must have felt like to hold me for the first time. I bet it was a mixture of love and fear, and disbelief and awe. In a second you pictured the entirety of your future compressed in a bundle of seven pounds and one ounce. It must have been overwhelming. Or at least, that's how I imagine it.

I have yet to be a parent and I'm several years older than you were when you had me. I was your experiment, and I say that with lightness in my heart. Us three had to figure out this whole family thing together. That's kind of the deal with the first born, isn't it?

We've had thirty-five years of highs and lows, and in the midst of it all we're still here. Every difficult moment, every celebration of joy is what has brought us to this point in our lives. You didn't always get it right, but you got me here. And for that, I am forever grateful that I have gotten to do this life with you, and will get to until your very last breath.

Whatever life brings next, I hope that I continue to make you proud. I know you're my
corner always.

Te quiero mucho, ma y pa

I can't remember the first time I saw black dahlias, but I
remember how they made me
feel

my eyes were always drawn to the mysterious beauty of
their black petals both haunting and enchanting

when I learned how short of a time they're with us, it
made me love them all the more

from late summer to early fall I make it a point to seek
them and allow myself the joy of their beauty until winter
comes to take them away

recently I learned it takes about 100 days for them to
bloom and they only do so if the conditions are just right

yet when they finally arrive no one calls them late
bloomers, do they?

if a small flower can take its time to arrive to where they
need to be, shouldn't we have all the more reason to be
patient and do the same?

- late bloomer

Be courageous enough to be content with where life has you, without mourning the past or longing for the future.

Summer is closing and that means autumn comes soon.

If there's anything to be taken away from this collection it's this: life will always come at us in seasons; unpredictability is always guaranteed and the only thing we really ever have control over is how we choose to show up in different seasons of our lives.

This season for me has been one of reaping the gifts that I patiently sowed. But that does
not mean I stop sowing.

To have a garden in the mind that is always in bloom, you must work at it. Daily.

Everyday brings a new challenge: what can be planted today? What needs to wait until
the season changes? How do I slow down so I know to differentiate between the two?

May you have the wisdom and courage to show up even when it's hard. Even when you convince yourself not to. Spring and summer may be the seasons we aim for, but we cannot enjoy them without passing through autumn and winter. Don't be afraid of the transitions. Learn to embrace them and be transformed by them.

I'm journeying through those seasons with you. I'll see you there.

lizzy madrigal

Acknowledgements

It's hard to put into words the gratitude that I feel for everyone that has been supportive of my writing for the past couple of years. Every cheer and word of encouragement has not gone unnoticed, and for that I thank you.

I'll start with my family. When I shared my plans to return to school five years ago, not once did you hesitate to support me. To my parents, Elias and Betty, I know the timing of me being a student again may have come as a surprise, but you voiced your support every step of the way. I love you.

To my siblings Gisselle, Denise, Sofia, and Elias- thanks for always reading snippets of my work whenever I sent something your way. Your belief in me has been fuel during moments of doubt. I love you all.

To my friends Yesenia and Lizzete- Thank you for holding space for my vulnerability. Your presence and thoughtfulness throughout this process has been unmatched. I appreciate you always redirecting me back to who I am and what I am capable of.

To my friend (and co-author!) Drew- Thank you for reminding me that imposter syndrome has no place in my life. Your presence and encouragement is a gift I will always appreciate. I'm so lucky to be doing part of this writing journey with you.

To Loren and the Paperbacks & Co. community- I'm so glad you found me when you did- what divine timing! You've been part of my writing life since I decided to return to writing. Thank you for cheering me on.

To my professors, and fellow students/friends from

Emerson- You get it. You know the struggle and the reward of creating art. I did take a detour from popular fiction (haha oops) but I hope I am still making you proud. Thank you for your accountability.

To my amiga/book coach Davina- I'm so happy I jumped on a plane to Colombia despite never having met you. Thank you for what you do; you're the reason so many of us can call ourselves published authors.

And lastly, a thank you to myself for finally doing it. I've been wanting to write since I was eighteen years old and it took seventeen years to get here. Get comfortable saying it: you're a writer. I can't wait to see what happens next.

Lizzy Madrigal is a therapist and writer based in Orange County, CA. She is a graduate of Emerson College's MFA in Popular Fiction and has an MA in clinical psychology from Pepperdine University. She has co-written several articles for the mental health nonprofit IDONTMIND and her poetry has been published in Harness Magazine and Writerly Magazine. While her primary focus in the past has been writing fiction, she also enjoys writing poetry to help process and understand her emotions to the fullest capacity. With more than ten years of experience in the mental health field, she hopes to combine her loves of psychology and writing to create stories that will continue to inspire others.

You can find Lizzy on Instagram under the handle @ lizzymadrigal and follow her writing on Substack at lizzymadrigal.substack.com.

Headshot by Drew Valo. You can connect with him on Instagram @ahumandreaming.